MW01154231

～ Historical Figures of the Hispanic World ～

Get to Know
Bernardo
de Gálvez

Guillermo Fesser

Illustrated by Alejandro Villén

Translated by Joe Hayes and Sharon Franco

For Max, Nico, and Julia, because
every time I think of them a smile
comes to my face.

G.F.

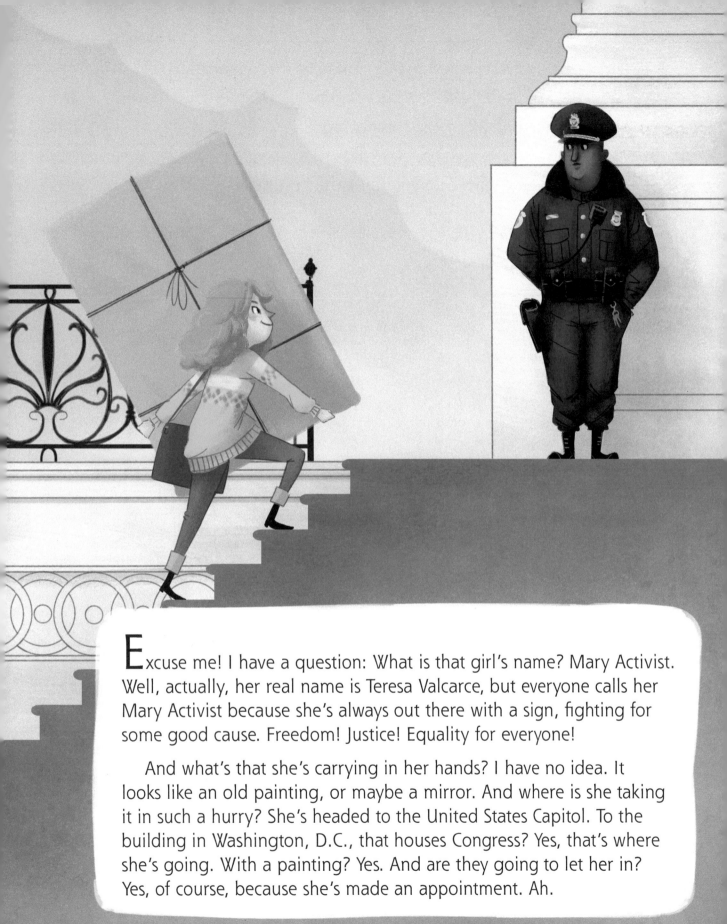

Excuse me! I have a question: What is that girl's name? Mary Activist. Well, actually, her real name is Teresa Valcarce, but everyone calls her Mary Activist because she's always out there with a sign, fighting for some good cause. Freedom! Justice! Equality for everyone!

And what's that she's carrying in her hands? I have no idea. It looks like an old painting, or maybe a mirror. And where is she taking it in such a hurry? She's headed to the United States Capitol. To the building in Washington, D.C., that houses Congress? Yes, that's where she's going. With a painting? Yes. And are they going to let her in? Yes, of course, because she's made an appointment. Ah.

"Hi," Mary Activist greeted the Chairman of the Senate Foreign Relations Committee.

"How can I help you?" the senator asked.

"I came to hang this painting of Gálvez, this nice-looking Spanish gentleman. Where do you think the best place would be?"

"A painting of whooo...?"

The senator couldn't hide his surprise. He put on his glasses and moved his face closer to the canvas. The fellow in the portrait was wearing a bright red shirt—a little tight around the belly—and his head was covered with an elegant wig with white curls.

"It's a pretty painting," he replied at last. "The thing is, Mary Activist, we don't hang portraits of unknown people here in the Capitol. But I do, in any case, appreciate the suggestion. It was a real pleasure meeting you."

"Wait! You must help me," the girl pleaded. "Gálvez was a hero in the American Revolution."

"An American hero . . . who spoke Spanish?"

"Yes, and Congress promised to hang his picture."

Mary Activist pulled out a photocopy of a document that a history professor had found in the National Archives, dated 1783. The members of Congress had promised to hang a portrait of Bernardo de Gálvez in the Capitol and . . . they still hadn't done it! The senator did the math. He couldn't believe it! But by now more than . . . two hundred and thirty years had gone by!

BY THE
UNITED STATES OF AMERICA
IN CONGRESS ASSEMBLED.
A PROCLAMATION,
1783

WASHINGTON •
D.C.

MÁLAGA •

14

"And you, how did you come to know all this?"

"It's because I grew up in Málaga, the province in Spain where Gálvez was born. And since I live in Washington, D.C. now, I decided to bring the painting here myself."

"Is this painting from 1783?"

"Oh, no! The original was lost many years ago, while waiting to be hung. This is a copy made by a different painter from Málaga. But so what? It's well done. The artist even painted it without going outside the lines. Do you want me to tell you the story of Gálvez?"

"If you would, please," the senator said, taking a seat.

Mary Activist pulled a piece of paper from her pocket. She cleared her throat, *ahem, ahem*. She put on a very serious voice, and began, "Spanish Iberico ham for a sandwich, detergent, and gym socks . . ."

"Whaaat?"

"Oh, excuse me!" she said. "Instead of my notes about Gálvez, I brought my shopping list. Oh, well, it doesn't matter. I'll tell you all about him without the piece of paper."

Don't tell me that Mary Activist could tell the whole story without having to read it. Yes, and by heart, too. The whole thing? You'll see.

"It turns out that in colonial times, Spanish was spoken in most of the territory that is now part of the United States. The first American cowboys were actually called *vaqueros*. That's where the word 'buckaroos' comes from, and the reason why cowboys still use Spanish words like ranch, lasso, corral, and rodeo."

"That is true. You're absolutely right."

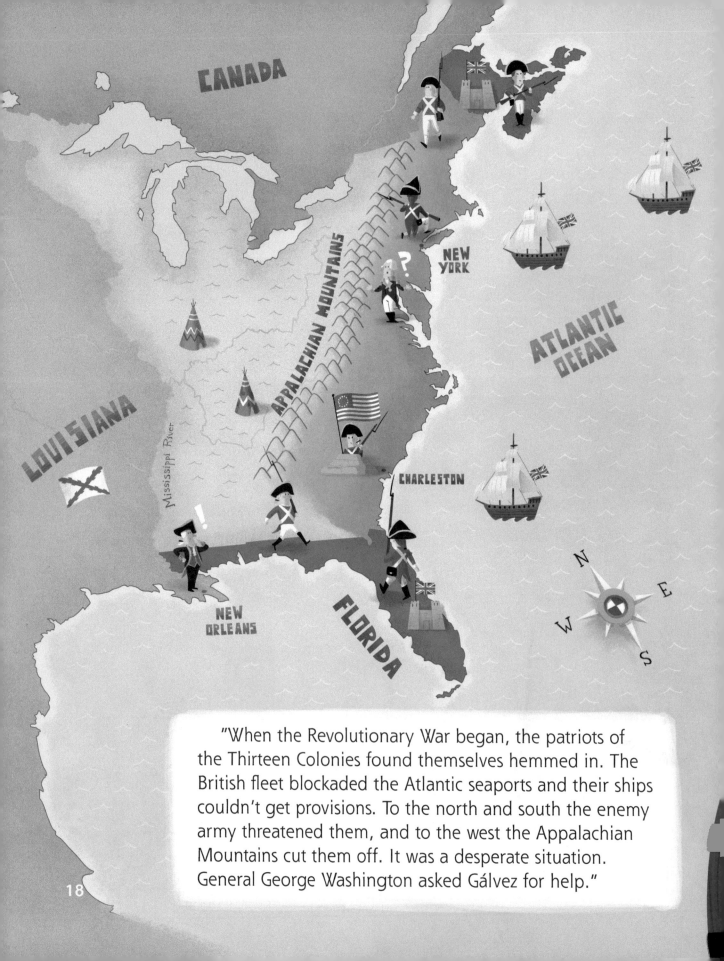

"When the Revolutionary War began, the patriots of the Thirteen Colonies found themselves hemmed in. The British fleet blockaded the Atlantic seaports and their ships couldn't get provisions. To the north and south the enemy army threatened them, and to the west the Appalachian Mountains cut them off. It was a desperate situation. General George Washington asked Gálvez for help."

18

"Are you sure of that?"

"You see, Gálvez was the governor of Louisiana, which at that time was a huge Spanish domain. It stretched from the Mississippi River to the Rocky Mountains and from the Gulf of Mexico to Canada. Imagine! Its capital was New Orleans, and to help Washington, Gálvez sent boats up the Mississippi River loaded with rifles, uniforms, food, blankets, and medicine."

"Great! Long live Bernardo de Gálvez!"

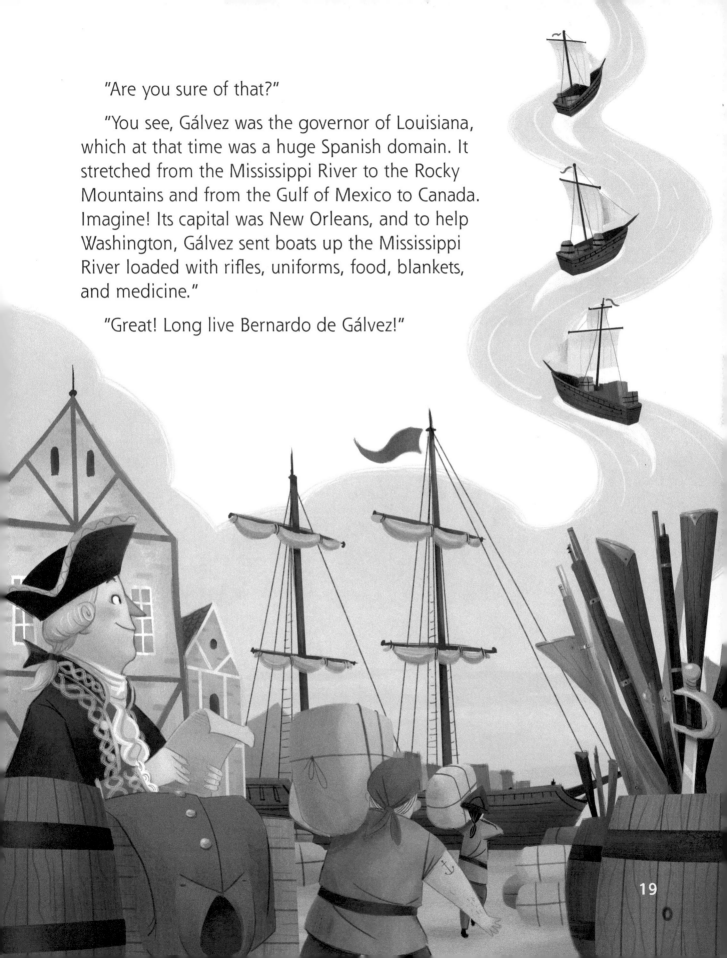

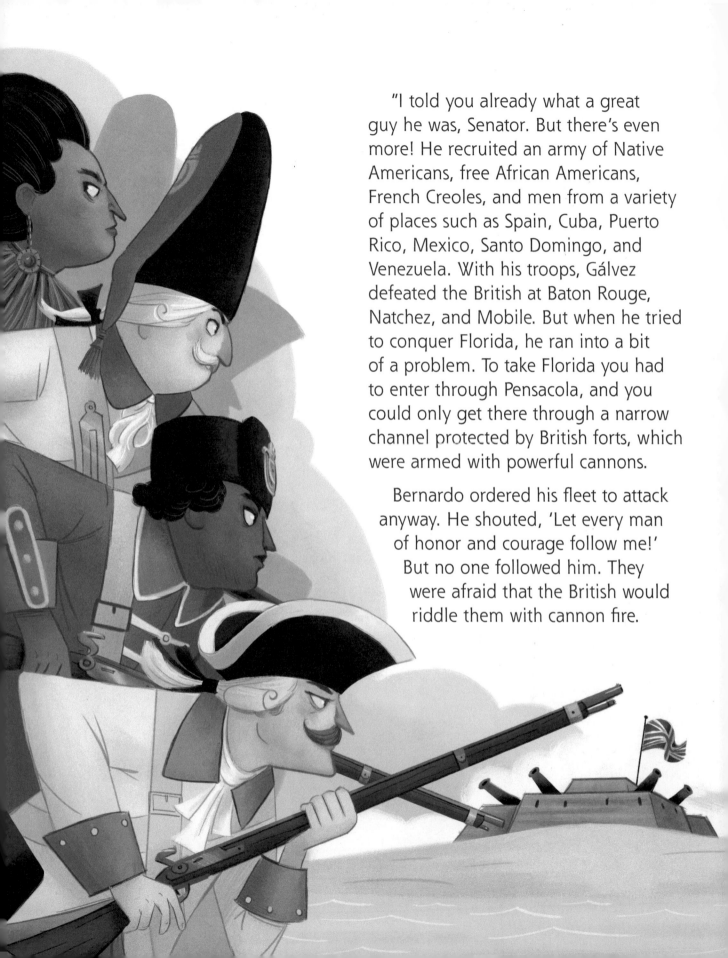

"I told you already what a great guy he was, Senator. But there's even more! He recruited an army of Native Americans, free African Americans, French Creoles, and men from a variety of places such as Spain, Cuba, Puerto Rico, Mexico, Santo Domingo, and Venezuela. With his troops, Gálvez defeated the British at Baton Rouge, Natchez, and Mobile. But when he tried to conquer Florida, he ran into a bit of a problem. To take Florida you had to enter through Pensacola, and you could only get there through a narrow channel protected by British forts, which were armed with powerful cannons.

Bernardo ordered his fleet to attack anyway. He shouted, 'Let every man of honor and courage follow me!' But no one followed him. They were afraid that the British would riddle them with cannon fire.

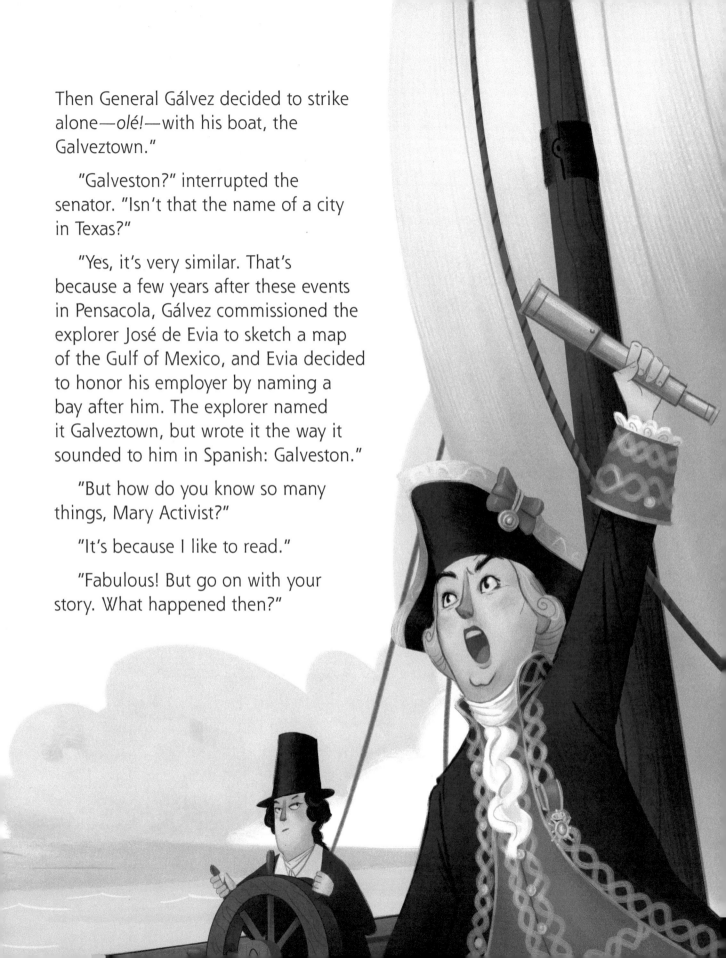

Then General Gálvez decided to strike alone—*olé!*—with his boat, the Galveztown."

"Galveston?" interrupted the senator. "Isn't that the name of a city in Texas?"

"Yes, it's very similar. That's because a few years after these events in Pensacola, Gálvez commissioned the explorer José de Evia to sketch a map of the Gulf of Mexico, and Evia decided to honor his employer by naming a bay after him. The explorer named it Galveztown, but wrote it the way it sounded to him in Spanish: Galveston."

"But how do you know so many things, Mary Activist?"

"It's because I like to read."

"Fabulous! But go on with your story. What happened then?"

"*Boom! Boom!* Twenty-seven cannon shots were fired at the *Galveztown*, and one by one he dodged them all. Inspired by their commander's courage, the rest of the fleet followed him. The British surrendered and the King of Spain granted Bernardo the honor of including the motto 'I ALONE' (*YO SOLO* in Spanish) on his coat of arms. Not satisfied with this, Gálvez asked his fellow citizens from Málaga to send money to George Washington to fund what would be his final battle, the Battle of Yorktown."

"And did they respond to the call?"

"Did they ever! The people of Málaga sent the money they had raised for the construction of their cathedral."

The senator clapped. "That's marvelous!"

"As a result, only one of the two towers was built, and that cathedral was thereafter referred to as the one-armed church."

"What an impressive story! All right, let's go."

"Let's go? Where?" Mary Activist asked in surprise.

"To the nearest hardware store. To buy a nail and a hammer to hang the portrait in the Capitol right away. This Gálvez is magnificent! He's a hero of the American Revolution, and the United States doesn't forget its heroes!"

"Bravo!" shouted Mary Activist. "And . . . um, Senator?"

"Yes?"

"Since we're going shopping, do you think we could stop somewhere for some ice cream?"

In the Senator's office, quietly waiting for them, sat the portrait of Bernardo de Gálvez, a hero of the American Revolution who spoke Spanish. Many people from the Hispanic culture contributed to the creation of the United States—many! And in recognition of them all, the portrait of Bernardo de Gálvez was finally going to hang in the Capitol. Shortly after the hanging of the portrait, President Barack Obama would grant the General honorary American citizenship.

Alfonso Vásquez | | 19.12.2014 | 05:00

The US Adopts Bernardo de Gálvez

And that's why the Chairman of the Senate Foreign Relations Committee, who was grateful to Mary Activist for helping him correct this historical oversight, treated her to a cup of strawberry ice cream—two scoops, topped with chocolate sprinkles and candied walnuts. It was wonderful! I'm not kidding.

Guillermo talks about Gálvez

What did you think of this story? To tell you the truth, even though I already knew it, I got excited about it all over again. You see, up until now, I had no idea that the language and culture of those of us who speak Spanish were so important in the creation of the United States. So, when I heard for the first time about the deeds of Gálvez, my eyebrows shot up and my eyes went as round as dinner plates. I was so surprised that, do you know what I'm doing now? I am spending a lot of time researching other traces of Hispanic heritage in the United States. All over. Like a detective. Just like that.

I go on the Internet, read books, talk to professors, and write to friends and family who live in other states. And so, little by little, I've discovered a few things. For example: The oldest city in the United States is named *San Agustín* (Saint Augustine in English). The first synagogue in New York was founded by a man named Luis Gómez. The herds of wild horses that live on the beaches of Maryland and Virginia come from the sinking of a Spanish galleon. So, if you discover something else, please pass it on to me. In exchange, I'll share more secrets about Gálvez with you.

Bernardo was born on July 23, 1746, in Macharaviaya, a village in the Province of Málaga in the south of Spain. When he grew up, he became a soldier. Since he soon stood out in the army for his courage, the king named him captain and sent him to patrol the Spanish domains of North America. He did it on horseback, with a leather vest and broad-brimmed hat, riding with his soldiers from one presidio to another. Ah, let me tell you something curious. Even though presidio means prison in Spanish, these forts were actually called this because they were meant to preside over, I mean to oversee, the Spanish areas of influence. Do you get it? Perfect!

Then, when Gálvez was promoted to be Governor of Louisiana, he aligned himself with the patriots, as you know. Washington appreciated his invaluable help so much that on the day George was inaugurated as the first President of the United States, in tribute of Bernardo, who had already passed away, the *Galveztown* was in charge of firing the thirteen-gun salute of honor—thirteen cannon shots that rumbled throughout New York from his ship docked in the bay. Sometimes I think I can still hear the echo: *boom, boom, boom...*

YO SOLO

Glossary

activist: a person that practices vigorous action or involvement to achieve political or social goals

align: to be on the same side as; to give support to

archives: collection of historical documents

cathedral: a very big church headed by a bishop

coat of arms: a shield or plaque with symbols that represent a person or a family

Creole: Original use: a person with European parents who was born in the New World. Modern use in Louisiana: a person of mixed African and European descent.

desperate: very hard or impossible to deal with

domain: land governed by a ruler or government outside of the state's borders

elegant: very fancy

fleet: a group of ships under one command

fund: to supply money for a special purpose

galleon: a large Spanish sailing ship

hem: to surround in a confining manner

honorary citizenship: citizenship given to a foreign person out of respect, sometimes after they die

oversight: a mistake, a failure to notice or do something

presidio: a military base or fort

recognition: acknowledgment of something done or given

recruit: talk into joining an army, enlist

rumble: make a loud, deep sound, like thunder

synagogue: a Jewish place of worship

traces: small signs or clues

variety: a number or collection of different things

© 2017, Vista Higher Learning, Inc.
500 Boylston Street, Suite 620
Boston, MA 02116-3736
www.vistahigherlearning.com
www.loqueleo.com

Text © 2017, Guillermo Fesser

Editorial Direction: Isabel C. Mendoza
Series Design: Mónica Candelas
Layout: Claudia Baca
Illustrations: Alejandro Villén
Translation: Joe Hayes and Sharon Franco

Loqueleo is part of the **Santillana Group**, with offices in the following
countries:

ARGENTINA, BOLIVIA, BRAZIL, CHILE, COLOMBIA, COSTA RICA, DOMINICAN REPUBLIC,
ECUADOR, EL SALVADOR, GUATEMALA, MEXICO, PANAMA, PARAGUAY, PERU,
PORTUGAL, PUERTO RICO, SPAIN, UNITED STATES, URUGUAY, AND VENEZUELA

Get to Know Bernardo de Gálvez
ISBN: 9781682921449

Published in the United States of America.

1 2 3 4 5 6 7 8 9 GP 28 27 26 25 24 23